IS MUHAMMAD IN THE BIBLE?

WHAT DOES THE INJEEL SAY ABOUT THE PROPHET OF ISLAM?

BY FOUAD MASRI

IS MUHAMMAD IN THE BIBLE?

Fouad Masri
P.O. Box 50986, Indianapolis, IN 46250
www.unlockthetruth.net
317.410.4492

ISBN: 978-1-944590-07-9

Layout design by Wesleyan Publishing House.
Cover art by Alesa Bahler/Legacy Design.
Production design by Niddy Griddy Design, Inc.

Quotations from the Qur'an are taken from The Qur'an Translation, 27th US Edition, by Abdullah Yusuf Ali (Elmhurst, NY: Tahrike Tarsile Qur'an, Inc., 2011).

Printed in the United States of America

DEDICATION

To all who respect the messengers of God

ACKNOWLEDGEMENTS

I am indebted to the many people who have helped me to accomplish this project, and I appreciate their assistance. I would like to thank my editor Julia, my publisher Karen and the BookVillages team, and proofreaders Bassam, Nancy, and Betsy.

Most of all I would like to thank my wife Lisa and my children. Without their support I would not have been able to finish this timely project. I am thankful for your help!

AUTHOR'S NOTE: VALIDITY OF THE INJEEL

In my book *Is the Injeel Corrupted?* I talked about my search for the truth of the Injeel.

I looked in the Qur'an to see what it says about the Injeel. In Surah 3:2-4 it says that God sent down the Injeel as His word, and in Surah 2:136 it says that Muslims must read and believe in the Injeel.

I did further research, and in the end I determined that the Injeel is a valid source of truth. References from the Injeel will be used throughout this book.

If you are interested in how I came to my conclusions, I recommend that you check out my book, *Is the Injeel Corrupted?*

–Fouad Masri

CHAPTER 1

المقدمة

INTRODUCTION

Today, more than ever, Christians and Muslims are interacting on a daily basis. The 21st century, with its technology, travel, and information superhighway, has become a forum for daily interactions between people from different cultures and religions.

Many Muslims today ask, "What does the Injeel say about Muhammad?" On the other hand, many Christians would like to know about Muhammad and the position they should take on his life and teachings. This book is my humble presentation of my research on the life of Muhammad and his teachings in comparison to the teachings of the Messiah Jesus.

I invite you to read this book; in it I present to you the commands of the Injeel in relation to those of Muhammad, the prophet of Islam.

CHAPTER 2

شهادة القرآن الكريم
THE QUR'ANIC WITNESS

WHAT DOES THE QUR'AN SAY ABOUT THE PROPHET MUHAMMAD?

Muhammad Is Just a Man

"Muhammad is no more than a Messenger: many were the Messengers that passed away before him. If he died or were slain, will you then turn back on your heels?"

Surah 3:144a

Muhammad Is Just a Messenger

"Muhammad is not the father of any of your men, but (he is) the Messenger of God, and the Seal of the Prophets: and God has Full Knowledge of All Things."

Surah 33:40

Muhammad Never Did Any Miracles

"Yet they say: 'Why are not Signs sent down to him from his Lord?' Say: 'The Signs are indeed with God: and I am indeed a clear warner.'"

Surah 29:50

Muhammad Is Not the Savior

"Behold! the angels said: 'O Mary! God gives you glad tidings of a Word from Him: his name will be Christ Jesus, the son of Mary, held in honor in this world and the Hereafter and of (the company of) those nearest to God...'"

Surah 3:45

In this verse, Jesus the Son of Mary (not Muhammad) is named as the one who will intercede on Judgment Day.

Muhammad Is Dead

"Every soul shall have a taste of death: and We test you by evil and by good by way of trial. To Us must you return."

Surah 21:35

"Truly you will die (one day), and truly they (too) will die (one day). In the End you will (all), on the Day of Judgment, settle your disputes in the presence of your Lord."

Surah 39:30-31

"Say: 'O men! I am sent to you all, as the Messenger of God, to Whom belongs the dominion of the heavens and the earth: there is no god but He: it is He that gives both life and death. So believe in God and His Messenger, the unlettered Prophet, who believes in God and His Words: follow him that (so) you may be guided.'"

Surah 7:158

The Qur'an does not give many details about Muhammad, the prophet of Islam. All sources about Muhammad's life are Muslim sources. Information on the life of Muhammad comes to us today from Islamic traditions and Muslim historians. The most common source is al-Hadith al-Sharif. It is a collection of stories and sayings attributed to Muhammad; they were selected by different writers and collected in multiple volumes of works. The most famous are Sahih al-Bukhari.

Although the stories of the life of Muhammad were gathered around 100 years after Muhammad's death, they were not collected into written volumes until 300 years after he died. Al-Hadith al-Sharif is elevated by many to be as worthy of study as the Qur'an. However, in the last fourteen centuries, Muslim scholars and religious leaders continue to disagree with and debate about the validity and authority of some of these sayings.

From this research, I will state what Islam, the Qur'an, and the Hadith teach about Muhammad, the son of Abd Allah, called the Prophet of Islam.

Islam claims that the Qur'an is the word of God, and that Muhammad is just a messenger. The Qur'an says that the Prophet of Islam was sent as a mercy to the world, but he is not the redeemer of mankind.

CHAPTER 3

شهادة القرآن الكريم

MUHAMMAD IN ISLAM

WHAT DO MUSLIM SCHOLARS BELIEVE ABOUT MUHAMMAD?

This chapter will give a quick synopsis about how Muslims view Muhammad Abd-Allah, the prophet of Islam.

Although, the Qur'an elevates Jesus (called the Word of God) and respects Muhammad. In contrast, Islam elevates Muhammad and respects Jesus.

Almost all the descriptions about Muhammad and his life come from al-Hadith al-Sharith. Although there are no independent historical sources outside of Islam, Muslim scholars today claim the following about the Prophet of Islam, Muhammad.

Islam claims: Muhammad Was a Great General

Muslim scholars claim that Muhammad led many raids and battles against those who refused to believe in Islam. Muslim sources claim these raids and battles prove that Muhammad was a great general and warrior. Although Muhammad lost some and won others, Muslim historians always emphasize the battles that Muhammad won.

Islam claims: Muhammad Was a Great Husband

Although Christians in Arabia refused to practice polygamy, Muhammad the Prophet of Islam practiced polygamy after the death of his first wife, Khadijah.

The Hadith mentions twelve wives of Muhammad, that he married after, Khadijah died: Sauda bint Zam'ah, Ayishah, Hafsah, Umm Salamah, Zaynab bint Khuzaymah, Juayriyah, Zaynab bint Jahsh, Mariyah The Coptic, Umm Habibah, Safiyah, Maymunah, and Rayhanah.

The details of the life of Muhammad, his relationship with his wives, and his interaction with his family are not extensive. Still, most Muslims today are taught that Muhammad was the best husband, even in his complicated polygamous marriages.

Islam claims: Muhammad Was a Great Businessman
Muhammad worked for his first wife Khadijah, who was a wealthy widow in the city of Mecca. Some today claim that he was an honest businessman that won Khadijah's favor, and she asked to be his wife.

Islamic Banking practices derive their rules from the life of Muhammad as a successful businessman in Mecca and Medina.

Islam claims: Muhammad Was a Great Politician
Muslim historians have gathered multiple stories about the life of Muhammad where Muhammad was able to solve disputes between tribes and individuals. The Treaty of Hudaybiyya in 628 A.D. is the most famous of his actions; this treaty said that there would be ten years of peace between Muhammad's followers and the city, and that Muhammad's followers could have the opportunity to take a pilgrimage to Mecca. In 630 A.D. he and his converts returned and conquered the city in spite of the treaty. This was proof of his political skills.

The Qu'ran highlights the following:
1. Muhammad Asked for Forgiveness
Muhammad often asked God for forgiveness of sins.

> "God accepts the repentance of those who do evil in ignorance and repent soon afterwards; to them will God turn in mercy: for God is full of knowledge and wisdom. Of no effect is the repentance of those who continue to do evil, until death faces one of them, and he says: 'Now have I repented indeed;' nor of those who die rejecting Faith: for them We have prepared a punishment most grievous."
>
> Surah 4:17-18

2. Muhammad claimed Jesus is the Messiah

Muhammad considered Jesus to be the Word of God and the Messenger of God. The prophet Muhammad proclaimed to Muslims that they should follow the teachings of Jesus in the Injeel.

> "And in their footsteps We sent Jesus the son of Mary, confirming the Law that had come before him: We sent him the Gospel: therein was guidance and light, and confirmation of the Law that had come before him: a guidance and an admonition to those who fear God."
>
> Surah 5:46

Muhammad never claimed that he was the redeemer, or the one who could save people from sin. God is holy, and desires His people to be a holy people. The people of God must be obedient to Him, and show this obedience through faithful and continually righteous acts.

In both the Qur'an and the Injeel Jesus is declared to be the savior of the world. Jesus became the redeemer; Jesus was the Adha to redeem all races and all peoples. As you continue reading, the Injeel will give a clear view of the Messiah, Jesus, and of the prophet of Islam, Muhammad.

CHAPTER 4

صدق الله العظيم

LET GOD BE TRUE

WHAT DOES THE INJEEL SAY ABOUT THE PROPHET MUHAMMAD?

The Injeel never refers to the prophet Muhammad by name, nor does it contain prophecies foretelling the coming of a messenger for just one people group, the Arabs. On the contrary, the Injeel says that God accepts all people who choose to follow Him.

God Wants People to Repent

"The Lord is not slow in keeping his promise, as some understand slowness. He is patient with you, not wanting anyone to perish, but everyone to come to repentance."

2 Peter 3:9

Those Who Follow Christ Are Made New

"Therefore, if anyone is in Christ, he is a new creation; the old has gone, the new has come!"

2 Corinthians 5:17

Jesus Is the Only Savior

"Jesus answered, 'I am the Way and the Truth and the Life. No one comes to the Father except through me.'"

John 14:6

God Shows Himself to All People

"...What may be known about God is plain to [all people], because God has made it plain to them."

Romans 1:19

God's Ultimate Revelation Was in the Messiah

"In the past God spoke to our forefathers through the prophets at many times and in various ways, but in these last days he has spoken to us by his Son, whom he appointed heir of all things, and through whom he made the universe."

Hebrews 1:1-2

CHAPTER 5

وأرسلنا الانجيل هدى للعالمين

IS MUHAMMAD MENTIONED IN THE BIBLE?

In the twentieth century some Muslim scholars began an ineffectual or barren movement to find verses in the Bible supporting Muhammad as a prophet whose coming was prophesied in the Bible. The most common argument for this is Dr. Badawi's approach.

Dr. Badawi was an economics professor who decided to address spiritual and religious questions. He took two verses from the Bible out of context and used them to claim that the Bible predicts the coming of Muhammad. The verses were Deuteronomy 18:18 and John 14:25-26. Dr. Badawi claimed that Deuteronomy 18:18 and John 14:25 prophesy the coming of Muhammad.

> "I [God] will raise up for them a prophet like you from among their brothers; I will put my words in his mouth, and he will tell them everything I command him."
>
> Deuteronomy 18:18

Dr. Badawi, states that Isaac and Ishmael were brothers; he says their father was Abraham, the first to believe in God. Since Muhammad is the descendant of Ishmael, and Moses is the descendant of Isaac, then this verse it talking about a prophet that is to come in the future.

Dr. Badawi's logic falters since he does not make the correct connection on the origin of the Jewish people. The Jewish people are the descendants of Jacob, Isaac's son. The Arabs are descendants of Ishmael and Esau. This makes them *cousins* of the Ishmaelites, rather than brothers; for that they would have to be direct descendants of Ishmael. When the verse says "their brothers," it is referring to the twelve brothers that were Jacob's sons; the descendants of those twelve are far removed from Ishmael's descendants. However, this verse makes sense if it is predicting the coming of Jesus. Jesus is descended from Judah, one of the sons of Jacob and grandsons of Isaac.

Dr. Badawi's error continues in his interpretation of John 14:25-26 in the Injeel.

> "But the Counselor, the Holy Spirit, whom the Father will send in my name, will teach you all things and will remind you of everything I have said to you."
>
> John 14:25-26

Dr. Badawi says that "the Counselor" (παράκλητος in Greek, written *parakletos* in English) mentioned in this verse is the prophet Muhammad. Dr. Badawi interprets the word *parakletos* as "a man... who was the Paraclete [sic], Comforter, helper, [and] admonisher sent by God after Jesus," and says that this is obviously a title of Prophet Muhammad.

This assumption is in error, since the word *parakletos* is more accurately translated "counselor"; moreover, this Being mentioned by Jesus lives in and powers the believer. The same word, *parakletos*, is used in another place in the book of John:

> "And I will ask the Father, and he will give you another Counselor to be with you forever – the Spirit of truth. The world cannot accept him, because it neither sees him nor knows him. But you know him, for he lives with you and will be in you."
>
> John 14:16-17

This *parakletos*, translated "the Counselor," is referred to as the Holy Spirit, namely the Spirit of God. Islam clearly teaches that Muhammad was just a man and that he does not live within any person; his role was to deliver a message. Thus he cannot be the *parakletos*.

Positive Teachings of Muhammad

Though Muhammad is never mentioned directly or indirectly in the Bible (Torah, Zabur, and Injeel), there are teachings of Muhammad that agree with the Injeel, and which most people think are good.

Muhammad Taught There Is Only One God

Muhammad taught everyone that idolatry is wrong, and all people should worship the one true God only.

> "Say: He is God, the One and Only..."
>
> Surah 112:1

Men and Women Are Equal in the Sight of God

Muhammad taught that men and women have equal religious responsibility in the sight of God. Muhammad taught that men and women were not equal socially, even though both have a personal responsibility to obey God.

"Men are the protectors and maintainers of women, because God has given the one more (strength) than the other, and because they support them from their means. Therefore the righteous women are devoutly obedient, and guard in (the husband's) absence what God would have them guard. As to those women on whose part you fear disloyalty and ill-conduct, admonish them (first), (next), refuse to share their beds, (and last) beat them (lightly); but if they return to obedience, do not seek against them means (of annoyance): for God is Most High, Great (above you all)."

Surah 4:34

"But those who believe and work deeds of righteousness, and believe in the (Revelation) sent down to Muhammad – for it is the Truth from their Lord – He will remove from them their ills and improve their condition."

Surah 47:2

Infanticide Is Wrong

Muhammad taught that people should not kill their children, especially their female infants.

"When news is brought to one of them, of (the birth of) a female (child), his face darkens, and he

> is filled with inward grief! With shame he hides himself from his people, because of the bad news he has had! Shall he retain it on (sufferance and) contempt, or bury it in the dust? Ah! what an evil (choice) they decide on?"
>
> Surah 16:58-59

> "When the female (infant), buried alive, is questioned – For what crime she was killed..."
>
> Surah 81:8-9

Muhammad Stopped Tribal Warfare

Muhammad brought peace to the land where he lived and stopped the constant infighting and retribution that hurt many people.

> "Verily We have sent you in truth as a bearer of glad tidings and a warner; but of you no question shall be asked of the Companions of the Blazing Fire."
>
> Surah 2:119

Muhammad United the Tribes

Muhammad unified the people around him though his leadership and teachings.

> "And hold fast, all together, by the Rope which God (stretches out for you), and be not divided among yourselves; and remember with gratitude God's favor on you; for you were enemies and He joined your hearts in love, so that by His grace, you became brethren; and you were on the brink of the Pit of Fire, and He saved you from it. This God makes His Signs clear to you: that you may be guided."
>
> Surah 3:103

Islam today presents an extensive and detailed report on the life of Muhammad. This report is based on the Qur'an, the holy book of Islam; on al-Hadith, traditions about the life of Muhammad; and on traditional folklore and beliefs about the life of the prophet Muhammad. Many of these references are hearsay, apocryphal, or pure fiction. Some stories from common folklore claimed that Muhammad performed miracles and healings; however the Qur'an, the holy book of Islam, does not affirm this claim.

The prophet himself and the teachings of Islam never claim that Muhammad can forgive sins. He is never declared a redeemer or savior of people. The prophet always asked for forgiveness and sought the mercy of God.

In contrast, Jesus the Messiah repeatedly was called the savior of the world (John 4:42; Acts 13:23; Philippians 3:20; 2 Timothy 1:10; etc.). John the Baptist called him the Lamb of God that redeems the sins of the world (John 1:29, 36).

CHAPTER 6

وأرسلنا الانجيل هدى للعالمين

THE PROPHET OF ISLAM AND THE INJEEL

Muhammad is never mentioned by name in the Bible. The Bible was written many years before Muhammad came, and there are no prophecies about him or verses that mention his name in the Injeel. However, the Injeel does talk about how people should judge the teachers claiming to speak the truth.

Jesus said that false prophets and deceitful religious leaders will come after him.

> "Jesus answered: 'Watch out that no one deceives you. For many will come in my name, claiming, "I am the Messiah," and will deceive many...

> and many false prophets will appear and deceive many people.'"
>
> Matthew 24:4-5, 11

> "Watch out for false prophets. They come to you in sheep's clothing, but inwardly they are ferocious wolves. By their fruit you will recognize them. Do people pick grapes from thornbushes, or figs from thistles? Likewise, every good tree bears good fruit, but a bad tree bears bad fruit. A good tree cannot bear bad fruit, and a bad tree cannot bear good fruit... Thus, by their fruit you will recognize them."
>
> Matthew 7:15-18, 20

The way you can judge whether or not those leaders speak truth from God is whether or not what they say agrees with Jesus' teachings and if it is in obedience to God.

> "Whoever says, 'I know [God],' but does not do what he commands is a liar, and the truth is not in that person. But if anyone obeys his word, love for God is truly made complete in them. This is how we know we are in him: whoever claims to live in him must live as Jesus did."
>
> 1 John 2:4-6

Jesus warned about false teachers and prophets who would contradict his teachings. We must look and see whether Jesus' and Muhammad's messages agree. The next chapter examines how Jesus' and Muhammad's teachings compare to each other.

CHAPTER 7

و لا غالب الا الله

THE PROPHET AND THE SAVIOR

MUHAMMAD AND JESUS

WHAT DID MUHAMMAD COME TO DO?

Muhammad Came to Declare the Message

"The Messenger's duty is but to proclaim (the Message). But God knows all that you reveal and you conceal."

Surah 5:99

"O Messenger! Proclaim the (Message) which has been sent to you from your Lord. If you did not, you would not have fulfilled and proclaimed His Mission. And God will defend you from men (who mean mischief). For God guides not those who reject faith."

Surah 5:67

"Those who follow the Messenger, the unlettered Prophet, whom they find mentioned in their own (Scriptures) – in the Law and the Gospel – for he commands them what is just and forbids them what is evil; he allows them as lawful what is good (and pure) and prohibits them from what is bad (and impure); he releases them from their heavy burdens and from the yokes that are upon them. So it is those who believe in him, honor him, help him, and follow the Light which is sent down with him – it is they who will prosper."

Surah 7:157

The only duty of the Messenger is to deliver the Message: there is only one God.

What Did Jesus Come to Do?

Jesus Came to Fulfill the Law

"'Do not think that I have come to abolish the Law or the Prophets; I have not come to abolish them but to fulfill them.'"

Matthew 5:17

Jesus Came to Call Sinners to Repentance
"On hearing this, Jesus said, 'It is not the healthy who need a doctor, but the sick. But go and learn what this means: "I desire mercy, not sacrifice." For I have not come to call the righteous, but sinners.'"

Matthew 9:12-13

Jesus Came to Speak the Truth of God
"'The Spirit of the Lord is on me,
because he has anointed me
to preach good news to the poor.
He has sent me to proclaim freedom for the prisoners
and recovery of sight for the blind,
to release the oppressed,
to proclaim the year of the Lord's favor.'"

Luke 4:18-19

"But he said, 'I must preach the good news of the kingdom of God to the other towns also, because that it why I was sent.'"

Luke 4:43

"'...In fact, for this reason I was born, and for this I came into the world, to testify to the truth. Everyone on the side of truth listens to me.'"

John 18:37b

Jesus Came to Save the Lost

"'For the Son of Man [Jesus] came to seek and to save what was lost.'"

Luke 19:10

"'As for the person who hears my words but does not keep them, I do not judge him. For I did not come to judge the world, but to save it. There is a judge for the one who rejects me and does not accept my words; that very word which I spoke will condemn him at the last day.'"

John 12:47-48

Jesus Came to Do God's Will

"'For I have come down from heaven not to do my will but to do the will of him who sent me. And this is the will of him who sent me, that I shall lose none of all that he has given me, but raise them up at the last day.'"

John 6:38-39

How Do Muhammad's and Jesus' Legacies Compare?

Muslims view Muhammad as the perfect man, perfect Muslim, perfect leader, and perfect Prophet. In contrast, the Bible declares that Jesus is the Word of God, the promised Messiah, sinless from birth, who died and rose from the dead to save all creation.

Muslims view the prophet Muhammad as a great military leader who conquered Arabia and led the Arabs to the worship of the one true God. Muhammad died in 632 A.D., leaving the Muslim community without spiritual and political leadership. How did the Muslim community respond after Muhammad's death? How did the disciples of Muhammad behave after he died?

The Muslim community went through severe turmoil and many Arabs left the religion of Islam. Led by Abu Bakr, the first caliph, the Ridda Wars were fought over a span of two years to convert Arabs back to Islam. After Abu Bakr's death, Omar led the Arab army outside Arabia and conquered lands from present-day Iran to Libya. Omar was assassinated, and Uthman took over the army and enlarged the Muslim empire from Spain to India. Many call this the fastest spread of Islam. However, this was actually a whirlwind military campaign. The disciples of Muhammad behaved as emperors, kings, and generals of an expanding army and an expanding empire.

The Messiah, Jesus, claimed that He came to save sinners. His kingdom was not a kingdom of gold, silver, or weapons. On the cross, Jesus said, "It is finished." Christ as the redeemer and savior of humanity finished the task of paying for our sins and redeeming all people and all races.

Jesus was the message to us from God. His life, teachings, and miracles were clear communication from God. (Hebrews 1:1-4).

After the resurrection and ascension of Jesus, his disciples and followers spread throughout the known world proclaiming that the Savior had come, and that all people can receive salvation. Peter the fisherman was crucified proclaiming the message of hope. Stephen was stoned to death proclaiming the message of hope. James and Andrew died proclaiming the message of hope. John the disciple of Jesus died of old age in exile still proclaiming the message of hope.

The disciples of the Savior spread the message without any military campaign. The prophet Muhammad pointed to the worship of one God; Jesus the Savior changes the hearts of humans. Dear reader, the next two chapters are the most important chapters. They tell us how we can be saved from our sin.

CHAPTER 8

و لا غالب الا الله

ONLY JESUS SAVES

WHAT IS SO SPECIAL ABOUT JESUS?

Muslims around the world annually celebrate the feast of Al-Adha. This feast takes place on the tenth of Dhul-Hijat, a month of the Muslim lunar calendar.

The root word for “Adha” is the Arabic word “Dahiya,” which means “sacrifice.” The Al-Adha feast is also known as the “Feast of Sacrifice” or the “Great Feast,” “Id Al-Kabir.” In the Turkic world the Adha feast is known as “Qurbani.”

At the Al-Adha feast, many Muslims sacrifice a sheep or a ram to commemorate the holy event when God redeemed the son of Abraham. This incident is recorded in the Qur’an in Surah 37:99-111.

The Jewish religion also believes in this same holy event when God redeemed the son of Abraham with a ram. When Abraham was about to sacrifice his son, the angel of the Lord stopped him. Abraham looked, and saw a ram caught in the thicket by its horns. He took the ram and sacrificed it as a burnt offering. The full record of this event is found in the "Tawrat," in Genesis 22:1-19.

Although the Jewish religion does not commemorate this specific event with a feast, the same idea and meaning are included in the Passover that was given to them by Moses. Jews celebrate the Passover to commemorate the night that God spared the Jewish firstborn from being slain in Egypt. The angel of death passed over the houses of those who put the blood of a slaughtered sheep at their doorposts, without harming their firstborn. The Passover is recorded in the Tawrat, in Exodus 12:1-14.

Where Is the Christian Adha?

Since Christians believe in both the Passover and the Adha events, why don't they celebrate them? Is there a Christian Passover too? To answer these questions, we need to look in the Injeel and examine its teachings on the character of God and His plan for mankind.

The Injeel Teaches That God Is Love

God is the creator of the universe and seeks fellowship with His creation. God's joy and pleasure is to communicate with humans, the highest of creation, bestowed with both a mind and a will. The Injeel says:

> "God is love. Whoever lives in love lives in God, and God in him."
>
> 1 John 4:16

> "I (Jesus) have come that they may have life, and have it to the full."
>
> John 10:10

Since God seeks fellowship with humans, why is our world so far from God? Why do people feel separated from God? It seems as if a great gulf separates us from enjoying God and His love.

The Injeel Teaches That God Is Holy

God is holy and righteous and humans are sinful. Everywhere we turn we see the sinfulness of humans. Their actions are symptoms of the real disease: Sin. Sin is rebellion against God.

All humans have sinned. Sin is choosing our way instead of God's way. All humans fall short of perfectly obeying

God's standard and law. Since the days of Adam, all people have chosen to go their own way rather than to obey God. This disobedience is what the Injeel calls sin.

We have all sinned against God Almighty and cannot remove our guilt. A righteous God is holy and cannot fellowship with sinful people. The Injeel affirms that all have sinned against a holy God.

> "There is no one righteous, not even one; there is none who understands, no one who seeks God. All have turned away, they have together become worthless; there is no one who does good, not even one."
>
> Romans 3:10-12

> "For all have sinned and fall short of the glory of God."
>
> Romans 3:23

The Injeel Teaches That God Is Just

The Injeel continues to explain that sin is what separates us from our loving and holy God. God's holiness condemns sin. The very righteous character of God cannot accept sin. Therefore God and humans have been separated by a great gulf, which is sin. This separation from God results in spiritual death.

> "For the wages of sin is death."
>
> Romans 6:23

The wages of sin is death; all sinners must die. Sin has made a great gulf between the holy God and flawed humans. Humans need God like a light bulb needs electricity. A light bulb without electricity is dead, lifeless and aimless. Sin has separated humans from God and made us spiritually dead, lifeless and aimless.

> "For all have sinned and fall short of the glory of God..."
>
> Romans 3:23

God's justice compels Him to punish and destroy sin. We have sinned against God Almighty, and the penalty is death. God cannot forgive a sinful person until that sinful person's debt is paid. Mere good works such as fasting or giving alms to the poor cannot pay the debt by earning God's favor. Even our most noble acts fall short of God's perfect holiness and justice. Our best is not good enough to please a perfect God, which means every single person – even the best of us – has sinned and must be punished.

A criminal cannot redeem another criminal; simply put, all humans have sinned and fallen short of God's law. God's holiness and justice do not allow forgiveness without payment of this huge debt. We have chosen our own way and broken God's commandment, so we must pay the penalty. The penalty is separation from God.

The Injeel Teaches That God Is Merciful

God's mercy sought to provide an answer to this problem. God wants to fellowship with us, His creation, but sin has created a gulf between Him and us. Only a righteous person can cross over the gulf to God. However, we have already established that everyone has sinned and fallen short!

Everyone, that is, except Jesus Christ. The Injeel teaches that Jesus Christ is the only bridge between a Holy God and sinful humans.

WHY JESUS AND NOT ANYONE ELSE?

Miraculous Birth

The Injeel teaches that Jesus Christ was not the son of a human father, but was conceived in the power of the Holy Spirit in the womb of the Virgin Mary. He was the only person to be born of a virgin. Jesus Christ's birth was not a result of the will of man, but the will of God.

Jesus Christ is unique in his miraculous birth. No prophet or leader has been born from a virgin. All prophets claimed that they were just humans, while Jesus Christ claimed that he was the "Word of God" – "Kalimat Allah." God's power is responsible for this miracle.

> "But the angel said to her, 'Do not be afraid, Mary, you have found favor with God. You will be with child and give birth to a son, and you are to give him the name Jesus. He will be great and will be called the Son of the Most High. The Lord God will give him the throne of his father David, and he will reign over the house of Jacob forever; his kingdom will never end.' 'How will this be,' Mary asked the angel, 'since I am a virgin?' The angel answered, 'The Holy Spirit will come upon you and the power of the Most High will overshadow you. So the holy one to be born will be called the Son of God. Even Elizabeth your relative is going to have a child in her old age, and she who was said to be barren is in her sixth month. For nothing is impossible with God.'"
>
> Luke 1:30-37

Miraculous Life

Jesus Christ lived a life of purity and honesty. He was obedient to the laws of God throughout his life. Jesus Christ taught like no one else and miraculously healed every weakness and disease. He was sinless from birth and was considered the greatest teacher that ever lived.

> "Jesus went throughout Galilee, teaching in their synagogues, preaching the good news of the kingdom, and healing every disease and sickness among the people. News about him spread all over Syria, and people brought to him all who were ill with various diseases, those suffering severe pain, the demon possessed, the epileptics and the paralytics, and he healed them. Large crowds from Galilee, the Decapolis, Jerusalem, Judea and the region across the Jordan followed him."
>
> Matthew 4:23-25

Miraculous Death

Jesus Christ did not come to earth merely to be a good teacher or healer. He came to be the sacrifice of God. Jesus Christ is righteous, sinless from birth, and his death alone can pay the penalty. He came to redeem humanity from its fallen state. The Injeel clearly states that all have sinned against God and are in need of salvation. Salvation means to be pardoned by God because someone paid the penalty that we could not pay ourselves.

Jesus Christ is the only righteous one, and he willingly paid the debt we owe. Humans are dead in sin. Sin is the gulf that separates us from God. Jesus Christ was crucified, and died as a righteous sacrifice for the human race. Just as Abraham sacrificed a ram instead of his son, Jesus on the cross was the sacrifice to pay the penalty of the sin of all mankind. The sheep died so the son of Abraham would be set free. Likewise, Jesus died so we can be set free. For as God redeemed the son of Abraham with a ram, likewise God redeemed the world through Jesus Christ.

As Muslims sacrifice a sheep at Al-Adha, and the Israelites sacrificed a sheep during Passover in Egypt, so God made Jesus Christ the perfect sacrifice for our sins.

Jesus became the true Adha. He was the Lamb of God to lift away the sins of the world. John the Baptist (known as the prophet Yahya) prophesied when he saw Jesus.

> "Behold, the Lamb of God who takes away the sin of the world!"
>
> John 1:29b

Through Jesus Christ, God bridged the gulf that separated us from Him.

> "All this is from God, who reconciled us to himself through Christ and gave us the ministry of reconciliation."
>
> 2 Corinthians 5:18

The justice of God was satisfied, for the penalty of sin was paid. The mercy of God was satisfied, for humans have been redeemed by Christ.

Miraculous Resurrection

Jesus Christ paid the penalty for our sin, so we may have fellowship with God. Jesus Christ is righteous and did not deserve death. Jesus is the incarnate Word of God who became the sacrifice for our salvation.

Christ rose from the dead on the third day according to prophecy. Christ's resurrection proved that his sacrifice was acceptable to God.

> "For what I received I passed on to you as of first importance; that Christ died for our sins according to the Scriptures, that he was buried, that he was raised on the third day according to the Scriptures, and that he appeared to Peter, and then to the Twelve. After that, he appeared to more than five hundred of the brothers at the same time, most of whom are still living, though some have fallen asleep."
>
> 1 Corinthians 15:3-6

Christians around the world celebrate the Adha and the Passover in one glorious celebration of the crucifixion and resurrection of Jesus Christ. In English it is called "Easter" and in Arabic "Id Al-Qiama." This is the Adha and Passover come true!

These holy events were object lessons God used so we could understand true redemption. The Bible says that the blood of calves and sheep will not wash away sins and that all our good works are like filthy rags compared to God's righteousness.

> "All of us have become like one who is unclean, and all our righteous acts are like filthy rags; we all shrivel up like a leaf, and like the wind our sins sweep us away."
>
> Isaiah 64:5-7

No one can possibly pay the huge debt that is owed to God.

The good news is, God sent Jesus Christ to be the sacrificial lamb of God who takes the sins of the world.

Jesus Christ Is Our True Adha!

An illustration: a friend of mine asks me to watch his house while he travels and I accidentally destroy the furniture. However, before his return, I wash his car. Would that cover the cost of replacing the furniture? No! If I ask my friend to have mercy and forgive me for destroying his furniture, since I washed the car, is it acceptable? No!

Even if he forgives me, my friend still has to pay for new furniture. Likewise, our good works are not righteous enough compared to God's righteousness. Our good works will never erase sin, for we are expected to do good and obey God's commandments. Our sin insults God's righteousness, and only Jesus' sacrificial work can suffice. Only the Christian Adha covers the debt of our sin and bridges the gap.

The Christian Adha is available to everyone, for Christ came to save all people, of all nations and races. Through Christ we can cross over to fellowship with God and experience His love and redemption.

CHAPTER 9

تعرفون الحق و الحق يحرركم

WHAT DOES THIS ALL MEAN?

WHAT DO I DO NOW?

It is not enough to know that God has found an Adha for sin. Each one of us needs to receive this sacrifice in a personal and humble decision.

The following is how we experience God's forgiveness. We must repent and receive Jesus Christ as Lord and Savior in order to experience God's love and forgiveness.

Repentance is turning to God from our own sinful ways and receiving God's offer of forgiveness made possible by Christ's work on the cross (the Christian Adha).

> "If we confess our sins, he is faithful and just to forgive our sins and purify us from all unrighteousness."
>
> 1 John 1:9

God forgives our sins if we confess them because Christ paid the debt. The perfect justice of God demanded punishment. The mercy of God was shown in the Christian Adha. Forgiveness can be granted since the justice of God was satisfied. Forgiveness can be enjoyed by repentant sinners because Christ paid the debt.

Sin dwells within the hearts of every human being. The whole human race is in need of a "heart transplant," a new life that will change a sinner to a saint. The Injeel says:

> "For the wages of sin is death, but the gift of God is eternal life in Christ Jesus our Lord."
>
> Romans 6:23

The Christian Adha released us from spiritual death and offered us eternal life. God's gift of eternal life is in accepting Christ's sacrifice. We receive Christ's sacrifice by faith, trusting God to forgive us. Christ's sacrifice is free, yet priceless. We are to receive it by faith. We can do nothing to earn it ourselves.

> "For it is by grace you have been saved, through faith – and this not from yourselves, it is the gift of God – not by works, so that no one can boast."
>
> Ephesians 2:8-9

The gift of God cannot be enjoyed unless it is received. We receive Christ and his sacrificial work by a personal commitment to follow him.

> "Yet to all who received him, to those who believed in his name, he gave the right to become children of God – children born not of natural descent, nor of human decision or a husband's will, but born of God."
>
> John 1:12

Christ is seeking to enter our lives, cleanse us from sin and mend our broken relationship with God. Christ wants to be our Lord and Savior. Jesus says in the Injeel:

> "Here I am! I stand at the door and knock. If any one hears my voice and opens the door, I will come in..."
>
> Revelation 3:20a

Prayer is talking to God. We can pray to God wherever we are and whenever we want. To receive Christ's sacrifice, the Christian Adha, we are to pray to God and in faith, trusting God, know that we have salvation. Your prayer to God can be something like this:

> "Dear Lord, thank you for Your love to me. I ask Your forgiveness because of Christ's atoning death. I open the door of my life and receive Jesus Christ as my Lord and Savior. Make me a new person. Thank You for giving me eternal life. In Jesus' name. Amen."

Pray this prayer and ask Christ to enter your life, forgive your sins and restore your fellowship with God. If you sincerely asked Christ to enter your life, be assured that He did.

It is important to know that God's promises are true. If you opened the door of your life, and asked Christ to enter as Savior and Lord, he will not deceive you. The Injeel teaches that Jesus Christ is faithful to His promises.

> "If you remain in me and my words remain in you, ask whatever you wish, and it will be given to you."
>
> John 15:7

"Never will I leave you; never will I forsake you."
Hebrews 13:5b

"Jesus Christ is the same yesterday and today and forever."
Hebrews 13:8

"I know whom I have believed, and am convinced that he is able to guard what I have entrusted to him for that day."
2 Timothy 1:12b

"Being confident of this, that he who began a good work in you will carry it on to completion until the day of Christ Jesus."
Philippians 1:6

APPENDIX 1

TERMS

Abd Allah – the name of Muhammad's father

Abraham – a patriarch, called a prophet by Muslims

Abu Bakr – one of the Muslim leaders after Muhammad's death

Adha – atoning sacrifice

Ahmadiyah – an Islamic sect that believes Jesus swooned on the cross, rather than dying

Al-Adha – The Feast of Sacrifice

Al-Hadith al-Sharif – one of the most important hadith

the Bible – a book that includes the Tawrat, Zubur, and Injeel; it is the holy book of Christianity

Christ – a Greek word meaning "the anointed one"; it is the Greek translation of the Hebrew word for "Messiah," and is one of the names of Jesus, son of the virgin Mary; he was considered the Savior

Dahiya – an Arabic word meaning sacrifice

Dhul-Hijat – A month in the Muslim lunar calendar

Dr. Badawi – a contemporary Muslim scholar

Gabriel – one of God's angels, mentioned in both the Qur'an and the Injeel

God – the almighty creator of all that is and ever will be

Gospel – a word meaning "good news"

Hadith – written traditions of Islam

Id Al-Kabir – the Great Feast, another name for Al-Adha

Id Al-Qiama – a celebration of Jesus' resurrection; Easter

Immanuel – literally "God with us," one of the names of Jesus

the Injeel – the Arabic name of the Gospel of Jesus, a very important book that Christians call the New Testament

Isa bin Maryam – Arabic for Jesus Son of Mary; one of the names of Jesus

Isma`il – the Arabic name for Ishmael

Jesus – an important figure in the Qur'an and the Injeel

Jesus Christ – one of the names of Jesus; has the same meaning as Jesus the Savior or Jesus the Messiah

Joseph – husband of Mary, who was the mother of Jesus; but he was not Jesus' father

Kalimat Allah – Word of God; one of Jesus' names

Khadijah – Muhammad's first wife

Maryam – the Arabic name for Mary, the mother of Jesus

Messiah – word meaning the "Anointed One"; also the "Savior"; one of the names of Jesus

Moses – a leader from the past, named a prophet by Muslims

Omar – one of the Muslim leaders after Muhammad's death

parakletos – a Greek word (παράκλητος) translated "Counselor" in English; a name for the Holy Spirit

Passover – the Jewish equivalent of Al-Adha

Prophet – a messenger from God

Qur'an – the holy book of Islam

Qurbani – another name for Al-Adha

rasul – a title meaning "messenger of God"

Sahih al-Bukhari – one of the major hadith

Savior – one who saves others; one of the names of Jesus

Son of God – one of the names of Jesus

Son of Mary – one of the names of Jesus

Surah – a division of the Qur'an; equivalent to a chapter

Tawrat – the holy books of Moses, also called the Torah

Torah – the holy books of Moses, also called the Tawrat

the Treaty of Hudaybiyya – a treaty between Muhammad and the leaders of Mecca, guaranteeing peace for ten years and providing a way for Muhammad's followers to make their pilgrimage to Mecca

Uthman – one of the Muslim leaders after Muhammad's death

the Word – one of the names of Jesus

Yahya – John the Baptist, a prophet

APPENDIX 2

TRANSLATIONS OF THE BIBLE

The Injeel was originally written in Koine Greek, the language of the common people in the Roman Empire. Scholars have taken great care to translate the Bible's message into many languages so that people from all nations and backgrounds can understand it.

Some people might accuse translators of changing the meaning of the New Testament. This is very far from the truth. Committees of dedicated scholars ensure that every translation reflects the original Greek texts. Christians consider the Bible a holy book, handling it with respect and honoring the original manuscript in every translation.

In the final analysis, those who doubt the credibility of individual translations should consider studying Koine Greek in order to read the New Testament in its earliest form.

In fact, I did that myself. I found the study of the New Testament Greek manuscripts to be fruitful, and intellectually as well as spiritually satisfying. I trust you will find it the same.

If you are wondering whether or not the Injeel has been corrupted, then please read "Is the Injeel Corrupted?", another of my books. In it I examine the reliability of the Injeel.

APPENDIX 3

THE FIVE PILLARS OF CHRISTIANITY: WHAT EVERY CHRISTIAN BELIEVES

Did you know that Christians across the face of the earth are unified by five core beliefs? We call these the "Five Pillars of Christianity."

1. One God – Christians believe in one God.
"For even if there are so-called gods, whether in heaven or on earth… yet for us there is but one God, the Father, from whom all things came and for whom we live."

1 Corinthians 8: 5,6

2. One Savior – Christians are redeemed by one Savior.
"[Grace] has now been revealed through the appearing of our Savior, Christ Jesus, who has destroyed death and has brought life…"

2 Timothy 1:10

3. One Spirit – Christians are filled and empowered by one Spirit.

"But you will receive power when the Holy Spirit comes on you; and you will be my witnesses in Jerusalem, and in all Judea and Samaria, and to the ends of the earth."

Acts 1:8

4. One Message – Christians are unified by one message.

"Jesus went into Galilee, proclaiming the good news of God. 'The time has come,' he said. 'The kingdom of God is near. Repent and believe the good news!'"

Mark 1:14, 15

5. One Family – Christians are part of one family.

"There is neither Jew nor Greek, slave nor free, male nor female, for you are all one in Christ Jesus."

Galatians 3:28

APPENDIX 4

FIVE PRACTICES OF CHRISTIANS WHO ARE FOLLOWING JESUS

1. Obey the Commands of Christ

"Do not offer any part of yourself to sin as an instrument of wickedness, but rather offer yourselves to God as those who have been brought from death to life; and offer every part of yourself to him as an instrument of righteousness."

Romans 6:13

"'I am the true vine, and my Father is the gardener. He cuts off every branch in me that bears no fruit, while every branch that does bear fruit he prunes so that it will be even more fruitful. You are already clean because of the word I have spoken to you. Remain in me, and I will remain in you. No branch can bear fruit by itself; it must remain in the vine. Neither can you bear fruit unless you remain in me. I am the vine; you are the branches.

If a man remains in me and I in him, he will bear much fruit; apart from me you can do nothing.'"

John 15:1-5

2. Pray

"Rejoice always, pray continually, give thanks in all circumstances; for this is God's will for you in Christ Jesus."

1 Thessalonians 5:16-18

"And when you pray, do not be like the hypocrites, for they love to pray standing on the street corners to be seen by men. I tell you the truth, they have received their reward in full. But when you pray, go into your room, close the door and pray to your Father, who is unseen. Then your Father, who sees what is done in secret, will reward you. And when you pray, do not keep on babbling like the pagans, for they think they will be heard because of their many words. Do not be like them, for your Father knows what you need before you ask him."

Matthew 6:5-8

3. Study the Bible

"Continue in what you have learned and have become convinced of, because who know those from whom you learned it, and how from infancy you have known the Holy Scriptures, which are able to make you wise for salvation through faith in Christ Jesus. All Scripture is God-breathed and is useful for teaching, rebuking, correcting and training in righteousness, so that the servant of God may be thoroughly equipped for every good work."

2 Timothy 3:14b-17

"Do not merely listen to the word, and so deceive yourselves. Do what it says. Anyone who listens to the word but does not do what it says is like a man who looks at his face in a mirror and, after looking at himself, goes away and immediately forgets what he looks like. But the man who looks intently into the perfect law that gives freedom, and continues to do this, not forgetting what he has heard, but doing it – he will be blessed in what he does."

James 1:22-25

4. Have Fellowship with Other Believers

"And let us consider how we may spur one another on toward love and good deeds, not giving up meeting together, as some are in the habit of doing, but encouraging one another – and all the more as you see the Day approaching."

Hebrews 10:24-25

5. Testify to Non-Believers

"[Jesus] said to them, 'Go into all the world and preach to gospel to all creation. Whoever believes and is baptized will be saved, but whoever does not believe will be condemned.'"

Mark 16:15-16

"And whatever you do, whether in word or deed, do it all in the name of the Lord Jesus, giving thanks to God the Father through him."

Colossians 3:17

BIBLIOGRAPHY

Aland, Kent. The Text of the New Testament. Eerdmans; Grand Rapids, MI. 1989.

Al-Sira Al-Nabawiya al-sharifa Oral Traditions on the Life of the Prophet. by Ibn Shakir Al-Kutubi, published by Dar Hatum, Beirut, Lebanon, 2001

Armstrong, Karen. Muhammad: A Biography of the Prophet. USA; Harper San Francisco. 1992.

Asbab al-Nuzul Reasons for the Revelations. by Imam Al-Nisabouri, published by Dar Al-Kotob Ai-ilmiyah, Beirut, Lebanon, 2000.

Armstrong, Karen. Muhammad: A Prophet for Our Time. New York, NY; Harper Collins Publishers. 2006.

Badawi, Jamal. Muhammad in the Bible. 1982. IslamiCity.com. 19 Mar. 2013. <http://www.islamicity.com/mosque/muhammad_bible.htm>

The Bible: New International Version. Biblica Inc., Colorado Springs, CO. 2011.

Hourani, Albert. A History of the Arab Peoples. The Belknap Press; Harvard, MA. 1991.

Lings, Martin. Muhammad: His Life Based on the Earliest Sources. Rochester, VT; Innter Traditions International. 1983.

Marston, Elsa. Muhammad of Mecca: Prophet of Islam. USA; Grolier Publishing. 2001.

Masri, Fouad. Is the Injeel Corrupted?. Crescent Project; Indianapolis, IN. 2006.

Muhammad. The Qur'an. Trans. Abdullah Yusuf Ali. Tahrike Tarsile Qur'an, Inc.: Elmhurst, NY, 2011.

"Muhammad and Women". 2002. PBS.org. 16 Jan. 2013. <http://www.pbs.org/muhammad/ma_women.shtml>

Tafsir Al-Quran Al-Karim Commentary on the Qur'an. by Sayyid Abdallah Shobar, published by Al-A'la Corporation, Beirut, Lebanon, 1995.

Quran Explorer Inc. Quran Explorer. 2006-2012. 16 Jan. 2013 <http://www.quranexplorer.com>.

Watt, W. Montgomery. Muhammad: Prophet and Statesman. Oxford, UK; Oxford University Press. 1961.

HOW CAN I GET A COPY OF THE INJEEL?

IS THE INJEEL CORRUPTED?
RESPONSE FORM

- ❑ I would like a copy of the Injeel. Please send me one free of charge.
  Language preference:______________________________
- ❑ Send me an in-depth study on the teachings of Jesus.
- ❑ I would like to follow Jesus Christ as my Savior.

Name ____

Address ____

City ____

State____________________ Zip Code ______________

Country____

Phone ____

Complete form and mail to:

Crescent Project
P.O. Box 50986
Indianapolis, IN 46250
www.crescentproject.org/resourcesformuslims

Or via email:
info@crescentproject.org

During Eid Al-Adha, many Muslims sacrifice a sheep or ram to commemorate the holy event when God redeemed the son of Abraham.

BUT WHAT IS THE CHRISTIAN ADHA?

Learn from the Injeel why God required sacrifice in the New Testament.

Contact us to request a copy of *Adha in the Injeel* (Arabic/English).

To get more of these resources go to unlockthetruth.net or fouadmasri.com.

UNLOCK THE TRUTH

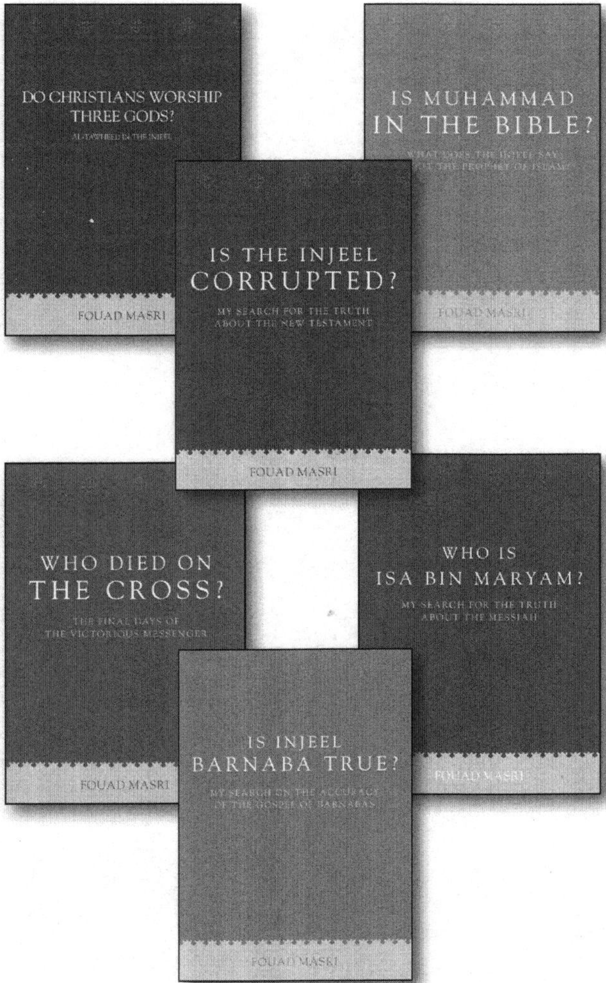

To order these resources, go to www.unlockthetruth.net.